What *to* Do When Counseling Fails

Jay E. Adams

TIMELESS TEXTS
Stanley, NC

© 2003 by Jay E. Adams
ISBN: 1-889032-43-3
All Rights Reserved

Printed in the United States of America

Contents

Preface

If you picked up this book on your own you probably are a counselor or a counselee who has experienced failure in counseling. Either way, I hope you will profit from what you read. I have tried to keep both sides of the human equation squarely before me when writing so as to make the volume profitable to everyone involved in flawed counseling situations.

Failure in counseling hurts. Hopes are dashed, people become discouraged, and problems may become all the more complicated. It hurts the counselee, the counselor, the church, and everyone who is closely related to the situation. It is important, therefore, to know how to detect errors, to know what to do to recoup from failure, and to learn how to avoid failure in the future.

The word "failure" must be understood. In biblical counseling we may view failure from two perspectives: the failure of the counselor, the failure of the counselee, or the failure of both. When the counselor or counselee alone fails, strictly speaking, there is no failure. Even if the counselee does not change in ways that he desired, there was success. How is that?

If, as in non-biblical counseling (or in some counseling wrongly called "biblical."), the goal of counseling is to bring about some desired change, and if the change does not take place all parties usually conclude that counseling failed. But in biblical counseling, the chief goal is *not* to bring about the desired change – as important as that might be – but to do those things that God requires in His Word. If one of the parties to counseling fails to meet God's requirements, but the other zealously does satisfy those requirements, counseling succeeds. In that sense, all proper counseling is successful *in God's sight*. And that is precisely what counts.

If the counselor or the counselee fails to do what pleases God we can rightly say, in the strictest sense, that the counselor or counselee failed.[1] Yet, sometimes, even when both the counselor and the counselee fail, if they both made a genuine attempt to fulfill God's requirements, but out of ignorance, because of misunderstanding, or from some other non-wilful reason counseling fails, good results still may arise out of the failure. How is *that*?

I am not talking about learning from failure – though there always is that possibility. But there is a third perspective beyond the two already noted to which I must call attention: God's perspective. God, Who sees the heart, knows the attitudes with which both the counselor and the counselee entered into and pursued counseling. And if these attitudes please Him, in His great mercy and goodness, He may yet overcome the failures so as to bring order out of confusion, righteousness out of sin, and joy out of sorrow.

God's overriding mercy and goodness in such instances, however, ought to lead both counselor and counselee to strive harder to learn and to do when they failed. The grace of God must not become an excuse for laziness or laxity but ought, rather, to act as a strong stimulus in learning and obeying.

Though there are various sides to failure, in this book I shall not rigidly distinguish between them. I shall look at counseling failure from all sides, including failure to honor God, failure to counsel or do as the Bible requires, and failure to achieve the changes that the Bible sets forth.

It is my hope that this volume will reach many at the point where, because of failure, they are ready to quit, and that it will not only instruct them about what to do instead, but will also encourage them to not give up.

---

1. Even if the desired change takes place. Sometimes God gives sinners what they desire even though it is not for their best. The fundamental desire of both counselor and counselee ought to be to obey and please God.

Chapter One
Checking Up, Not Checking Out

In the preface I said that failure comes in two forms: failure of the counselor and failure of the counselee, but that failure is not necessarily a total failure if either party did what God requires. So, one of the first things to determine is who failed – the counselor, the counselee, or both. The next thing is to discover why the failure took place.

The idea here is not to place blame, though in some cases there may be serious blame. Rather, it is to discover what went wrong in order to fix it if possible (it is not always possible). So I have developed a check list of fifty failure factors[1] to which one may refer in time of failure or to stem the tide when failure seems imminent. These are as follows:

1. **Is the counselee a Christian?** If not, there is no hope of success in terms of his reaching any biblical goal. Truly biblical counselors do not knowingly counsel non-Christians. God has not called us to help move a counselee from one lifestyle that is displeasing to Him to another that is also displeasing to Him. See also Romans 8:8: "Those who are in the flesh, *cannot* please God" [emphasis mine].

2. **Has there been genuine repentance on the part of the counselee?** If one has not confessed sin and received God's forgiveness (and forgiveness from anyone else necessary) there is little hope of pleasing God in any endeavor until repentance occurs.

3. **Is he vitally committed to the biblical change?** Commitment involves at least the following: a) an understanding of what should be done, b) a desire to do it in order to please God, c) willingness to obtain all

---

1. Similar to those found in page 797 of *The Christian Counselor's New Testament* (Second Edition). Some items have been enlarged, others omitted or added.

resources and skills necessary to pull it off, d) good planning, and e) action – following the plan.

4. **Are your agendas in harmony?** It is essential for the counselor and the counselee to agree upon *God's* agenda. Otherwise they will be shooting past one another.

5. **Have *all* of the necessary data been disclosed?** Counselors must be sure that they seek all; counselees must be certain that they are holding back nothing of importance.

6. **Is there someone working against the counseling?** Persons involved in sessions or outside of sessions, who are adverse to counseling, can be a great hindrance to success. This area must be investigated thoroughly in order to be sure that this question is properly addressed.

7. **Do both counselor and counselee recognize that God is in the counseling process?** That is to say, they both know that whatever takes place is done under the scrutiny of God and that any change in the right direction must be achieved by Him working through His Spirit and His Word.

8. **Would a medical examination be in order?** Timeless Texts publishes *The Christian Counselor's Medical Desk Reference* by Robert Smith, MD which helps Christian counselors determine when to recommend a medical examination.

9. **On what level is the counseling proceeding?** There is the level of *irritation* (what moved the counselee to seek counsel), the level of the *most recent occurrence* (of the problem), and the level of the *underlying pattern* of which the most recent occurrence may be only the latest in a series of events that, if not dealt with, will lead to more occurrences in the future.

10. **Are there other problems that must be settled first?** The problem may be complex. Have all factors been adequately explored? Sometimes a complicating problem, that must be dealt with first, may have arisen from an attempt to solve the presentation problem in unbiblical ways.

11. **Has dealing with the issue been uppermost and the relationship ignored?** Until persons at odds with one another have settled relational matters through confession and forgiveness, they will be in no condition to solve issues that exist between one another and God.

12. **Did the counselor give adequate scriptural hope?** Hope comes from the God of all hope (Romans 15:4,13). Does the counselee believe that God has provided the answers to his problems in Scripture? Scriptural promises are the foundation of true hope (v. 4).

13. **Did the counselor minimize the counselee's problem?** It is important for a counselor to take all negative comments that the counselee makes about himself seriously. Otherwise, the counselee will probably tune him out.

14. **Have speculative data been accepted as true?** "I guess that it is so because..."

15. **Has concrete homework been assigned from the initial session on?** Start out right by setting a pattern of expectation of change from the beginning. And remember, no abstract assignments should be given.

16. **Would using a DPP[1] form help?** Discovering Problem Patterns (DPP) may be critical to understanding patterns and dealing with them biblically.

---

1. A sample of the DPP form may be found in *The Christian Counselor's Manual*.

17. **Is the problem a life-dominating problem?** If so, total restructuring of the counselee's lifestyle will be necessary.

18. **Does the counselor empathize with the counselee's self-pity?** This will hinder progress; self-pity must be countered biblically.

19. **Does the counseling focus on problems or on solutions?** The focus on problems should continue only until they are understood and repentance is effected. Then, the focus should quickly shift to biblical solutions. Christian counselors are basically solution-oriented.

20. **Has there been a discussion of the counselee's language patterns?** Taking note of patterns of revenge, arrogance, hopelessness, and so forth may reveal a lot.

21. **Have counselees been allowed to speak negatively behind others' backs?** Gossip is forbidden in Scripture, as is "talking negatively behind someone's back" (James 4:11).

22. **Have new elements entered the picture since counseling began?** Often, these change everything. Awareness of this fact is important.

23. **Has the focus been upon the wrong problem?** Much time may be wasted by focusing upon wrong problems.

24. **Is the problem not so complex after all, but simply a case of open rebellion?** If so, say so and treat it as such rather than toning it down in any way.

25. **Have there been enough homework assignments?** Has the counselee become discouraged because counseling has not moved forward fast enough?

26. **Does the counselor have the same problem as the counselee?** If so, he probably will not be able to help until he solves his own problem.

27. **Does doctrinal error lie at the base of the problem?** Assurance, for example, may not be possible (shouldn't

be) for one who thinks it is possible to be saved and then lost.

28. **Do drugs, tranquilizers or significant sleep loss account for the problem?** All the effects of LSD may occur when one fails to obtain adequate sleep over several days.

29. **Has the "put off" been stressed to the exclusion of the "put on"?** Habit patterns must not only be broken but replaced by their biblical alternatives.

30. **Has there been adequate prayer?** Ask God to work through the counseling from His Word.

31. **Is the counselee "turned off" by the counselor (or vice versa)?**

32. **Is there a willingness to settle for something less than God's biblical solution?**

33. **Has fear made the counselor unwilling to face the counselee's problem biblically?**

34. **Has sin been called "sin" or something else?** Christ came to deal with sin. In that fact lies the hope of counseling. To fail to call sin what it is takes away hope.

35. **Does the counselee suspect that change is impossible?** Language of hopelessness is studded with such words as "I can't."

36. **Has the counseling been feeling-oriented rather than commandment-oriented?**

37. **Has the church, with all of its resources, been brought into the picture?**

38. **Is church discipline in order?**

39. **Are partially-fulfilled or unfulfilled homework assignments accepted?** If so, the counselor will be teaching his counselee to be irresponsible, and that God accepts shoddy efforts.

5

40. **Does the counselor know the biblical solutions to the problem?** If not, he should freely admit the fact and search out such solutions.

41. **Has the counselee been praying, reading Scripture, fellowshipping with God's people, and witnessing?** If not, counseling may be harmful rather than helpful.

42. **Does the counselor believe there is hope for this counselee?** If he doesn't, he may communicate this to the counselee and, thereby, only increase any doubts that the counselee may have.

43. **Would the help of another biblical counselor be in order?** If this is necessary, the counselor should refer both his counselee and himself. He needs to learn from watching a more experienced counselor.

44. **Would a full, rereading of the Counselor's Weekly Counseling Records disclose patterns, trends, failures, and so forth?**

45. **Has the questioning been intensive as well as extensive?** Every area of life should be explored extensively for possible problems and, when found, each potential problem area should be probed intensively.

46. **Have there been false assumptions about this case?** For instance, did you think that it is just like a previous case? No two cases are exactly alike. Adequate data-gathering must be done for each.

47. **Has the counselee knowingly or unintentionally twisted or concealed data?**

48. **Should other persons be brought into counseling sessions to assist?** They may be able to supply additional data, monitor the counselee's progress, and give different viewpoints?

49. **Does the counselee fully understand what he is to do?**

50. **Is radical amputation necessary before trying to learn new ways?** Old patterns may be difficult to "put off" apart from such an approach (cf. Matthew 5:29, 30).

Use this Space for Additional Items

While this list is not exhaustive, it does cover most of the reasons that counselors fail to help their counselees. But it is also of use to counselees. Often a counselee will unwittingly choose a counselor who does not use biblical methods, even though he may call them "biblical." Moreover, there may be failures on the part of the counselee that the checklist may uncover. Some of the items, as you can see, pertain to counselee failures and others to counselor failures.

I suggest that when there is a failure, or better still, when failure seems imminent, it might be wise to turn to this list to determine which item or items best describe what is happening. In this way, it may be possible to prevent failure or (in case it has already occurred) to discover why the failure took place. In this way similar failure in the future may be averted. Indeed, in order to prevent failure, you might run through the list before each counseling session. In all cases, it is important to have a biblically-based checklist of some kind.

Chapter Two
A Case in Point

You are not the only one who has failed. The apostles did too! In the case that we are about to study, the apostle John "failed" to achieve his secondary[1] goal in counseling. He did all the right things, so strictly speaking, it was the counselee, not he, who failed. Indeed, in like manner, there was an occasion when Jesus found it necessary to ask, "Where are the nine?" (Luke 17:17). Clearly he didn't fail; the nine out of the ten did. In order to facilitate our study of the biblical case in which John the apostle was involved, let us first read the short epistle of III John:

[1] The elder to my dear friend Gaius, whom I love in truth. [2] Dear friend, I pray that all your interests may prosper and that you may have good health, in the same way that your soul is prospering.

[3] I say this because I was delighted when the brothers came and testified about your truth, that you are walking in the truth. [4] Nothing pleases me more than to hear that my own children are walking in the truth.

[5] Dear friend, you are faithful when you do anything for the brothers – especially for strangers – [6] who have testified about your love before the church. You will do well to send them forward on their trip in a manner that is worthy of God, [7] because they went out on behalf of the Name, taking nothing from the Gentiles. [8] We, therefore, ought to take up the support of such men so that we may be fellow workers for the truth. [9] I have written something to the church, but Diotrephes, who loves the place of preeminence among them, doesn't recognize our authority. [10] For that reason, when I come, I shall remember everything that he has done; for example, the evil words

---

1. See the Preface concerning primary and secondary goals.

that he babbles about us! And as though that were not enough, he himself doesn't recognize the authority of the brothers, but stops those who want to, and throws them out of the church. [11] Dear friend, don't imitate evil, but imitate good. The one who does good is from God; the one who does evil hasn't seen God. [12] Demetrius has a good testimony from everyone, even from truth itself. We also give testimony to him, and you know that our testimony is true.

[13] I had much to write to you, but I don't want to do so with pen and ink. [14] Rather, I hope to see you as soon as possible and we shall talk face to face.

Peace to you. The friends greet you; greet the friends by name.

In order to understand this passage as thoroughly as possible, I shall go through it, explicating each verse. At the end of the chapter, I shall sum up the problems presented by this counseling failure. Then in the following chapters, I shall deal with each of these biblically to see what we can learn from them.

First, we must understand that all that we know about Gaius is found in this short letter. There are three other Gaiuses mentioned in the New Testament (Gaius of Derbe, of Corinth, and of Macedonia) but we are unable to identify this Gaius with any of them. The name Gaius was similar to our name "Smith" or "Jones." In fact, in sample documents, where today the name "John Doe" appears, in John's day they wrote in "Gaius." But what we learn of the man is outstanding. He was a close friend of John the apostle, in fact, one of his converts ("my own child," v. 4). He was "walking in the truth" (v. 3, 4). That means that his outward lifestyle exemplified those truths that the apostolic teaching enjoined upon Christians (today found in the New Testament). He may not have been financially well off, and his health may have been failing, but this isn't certain

(v. 2)[1]. At any rate, John takes a common greeting and gives it a new twist: he prays that Gaius' financial interests and his health may be as successful as his spiritual interests! With many of us today, he'd have to turn that around, wouldn't he? These words give us a clear indication of the high esteem in which John held Gaius. Moreover, Gaius had treated the "brothers" well. Clearly, his life was exemplary.

John had sent out some itinerant missionaries (the "brothers" of v. 3) and had given them authority to preach and teach in the name of Christ. John commends Gaius for his treatment of these missionaries. They, in turn, spoke well of Gaius when they returned to John and the church where he taught (probably at Ephesus). And Gaius is encouraged to continue to provide whatever necessities were needed to travel to the next Christian's home (v. 6). Indeed, as he does so, he is encouraged to entertain them and supply all that was necessary to meet their needs as if he were entertaining and supplying God himself (v. 6)! Then, John gives the reason: they took nothing from those non-Christians ("Gentiles") to whom they preached "for the sake of the Name." That is to say, they didn't want their hearers to think they were after money and thus defame the Name of Jesus Christ. So if they were to receive support as they traveled, it must come from Christians (v. 7, 8).[2] All believers who supported them would be counted "fellow workers for the truth" as if they were accompanying the missionaries (v. 8).

Then comes the problem. Diotrephes (probably the pastor of the church that Gaius attended) refused to receive the

---

1. The formula found in v. 2a was common in letters of the day. P. Oxyrincus 1680, for instance, has this salutation: "I pray to God that you are prosperous and successful and in good health." P. Oxyrincus 282 reads, "Before all else I pray that you may have health and the best of success." Plainly, John has taken a standard form and turned it into something significant!

2. An important principle, not always observed by churches today. The world should not be asked to support the work of the church through rummage sales, strawberry festivals, suppers, and the like.

brothers. And he declared that anyone who did would be disciplined out of the church. Presumably, Gaius was sitting on the curbstone outside, scratching his head in confusion and unbelief! "What did I do wrong that I was thrown out of the church?" he may have pondered. "I thought I did right in entertaining the missionaries, but here I am – out of the church!"

John tells Gaius that he had heard of the situation, explains by what he writes that he understood it, and tells Gaius that he wrote to the church of which Diotrephes was the pastor (v. 9). He also charges Diotrephes with "loving the place of preeminence," rejecting apostolic authority, and further exacerbating matters by speaking "evil words" and all sorts of nonsensical falsehoods against John and the brothers (v. 9, 10). John then assures Gaius he will deal with ("remember") Diotrephes when he comes.

Meanwhile, he shoots off this brief letter to Gaius, assuring him that he did well, and referring him to Demetrius, the bearer of the letter. He urges Gaius to imitate the exemplary life of Demetrius rather than that of Diotrephes (v. 11). Since Gaius did not know Demetrius, John testifies that he is a true brother who ought to be listened to and gives him an excellent character reference (v. 12).

He then closes this stop-gap letter, written on one piece of papyrus, doubtless, in order to meet the crisis with final words of greeting, saying he planned to come to see Gaius soon and then they could talk at greater length (v. 13, 14).

In brief, that is what III John is all about. Much more could be said, but probably what I have written will give you the gist of the epistle. Now what sort of problems in counseling are apparent? Let's sum up. We shall deal with each of these in the chapters that follow.

1. Diotrephes' rebellion, slander, and arrogance had to be addressed. Presumably, he had spread untruths about John and the brothers.

2. Church discipline was in order. This case was open, public and schismatic (a last stage matter). Only repentance by Diotrephes could stay the process.

3. Gaius needed further help along with any other members who had been wrongly ejected from the church. Many ancillary problems would have to be dealt with. Clearly, conflict resolution was called for.

4. Apostolic authority (which was Christ's authority) had been rejected. This, too, was a serious matter.

5. John had declared himself on the side of Gaius and the missionaries over against Diotrephes and any others who were siding with him. Taking sides, as he must, was important for the sake of peace and truth.

Plainly, there was much to do. Many threads were left dangling. John did all that he could until such time as he was able to visit Gaius and his church. But for now, Demetrius was sent to do what he could in John's name, with his complete, apostolic endorsement. This letter, itself, not only confirmed Demetrius' authority, but also assured Gaius that what he had done was proper in God's eyes and encouraged him to continue to imitate good. All in all, this letter must have gone a long way toward righting the wrongs that had been done, but it was not enough – Diotrephes still had the upper hand. So John was coming in the full authority of Jesus Christ to deal personally with him.

Chapter Three
Counseling by Mail

John says "I wrote something to the church, but...." Was it because he tried counseling by mail that counseling failed? No. Paul did the same thing – and succeeded: "I am not writing these things to shame you, but to counsel[1] you as my dear children" (I Corinthians 4:14). II Corinthians makes it clear that through his first letter, Paul was able to turn the Corinthian church around.[2] So it is not the medium that John used that was at fault. No, it was proper for John, when he could not go immediately, to write to the church (which of course included its pastor).

Mail in those day was much slower and often uncertain. There was a Roman post that (much like our Pony Express in years past) carried mail throughout the Roman empire. The problem was that only official, government mail was transported by this means. The average citizen found it necessary, therefore, to find someone who was traveling to the destination of his letter and entrust him to take it. There were many hazards along the way such as ship-wreck, pirates, brigands along the roads, and so on, that made reaching its intended destination uncertain. Then, there was also the problem of finding the person to whom the letter was written. Since he wasn't expecting it, he might be out of town or otherwise unavailable. Another problem was finding some trustworthy person who was traveling to the letter's destination in the near future. As a result, sometimes mail had to wait quite a while before it could be sent. All of these ancient hazards and difficulties had to be faced in using mail.

Obviously today we have no such inconveniences. With telephones, faxes, the post office, and E-mail we can reach

---

1. The word used is *noutheteo*, "to nouthetically confront."
2. By the power of the Spirit working through the inspired Word that he wrote, of course.

another almost instantly. This gives us a great advantage over John and Paul. But there are also some disadvantages. Before writing, if there was no one to carry the letter to its destination, one had at his disposal a great deal of time to ponder what to write. And if new information reached him in the interim, like Jude (Jude 3), he could change what he had intended to write. Probably, therefore, even short letters like III John took much longer to write than those that we dash off by E-mail, for instance. Though the letter was brief, John probably gave a great deal of thought to what to say and how to say it.

At any rate, one thing is clear: John did not receive the sort of response from his letter that he had hoped for. Diotrephes was an arrogant, self-centered, proud man. And his response (we don't know how it reached John, but it did[1]) showed it (III John 9, 10). Nor do we know how the church as a whole, or in part, responded to John's letter.[2] All we know is what we read in III John. The letter might have been effective among some members of the congregation if they had an opportunity to read it. But all of that is speculation, nothing more.

The letter to Gaius was, of course, a second letter of counsel. We shall see in it (as we proceed) that there are many elements from which we may learn how to counsel. But for now, let us certainly assume that it was effective. Gaius must have treasured and followed it (and perhaps others did so as well) because it has come down to us as a part of the New Testament.

Christian counselor, do you efficiently use the means that are at your disposal for communicating with counselees? If you only counsel in the counselee's presence, you probably miss opportunities to be of help. There are emer-

---

1. Possibly by letter or, more likely, by word of mouth from some other "brothers" who returned and told John about Diotrephes' reaction.

2. Or, for that matter, whether they even had opportunity to hear it read (Diotrephes was the sort of person who might have hidden it from them).

gency situations when you may not be able to meet together for counsel. Yet, a brief word by E-mail, or a phone call would be in order. The letter also still has a place (when sending longer materials, etc.) since not everyone has access to a fax machine. Let me encourage you to use one of the modern means of communication when:

1. checking up on a counselee's progress between visits (he may E-mail you information);

2. when encouragement is needed between sessions;

3. when you have heard that something adverse has happened;

4. when you might have to miss a counseling session;

5. when you are anxious to hear how something turned out.

There are many other occasions on which modern means of communication might (ought to) be used. Having mentioned a few to stimulate your thinking, I'll leave it to you to add other suggestions.

You have noticed, of course, that John wrote in a crisis situation. The brief letter indicates that John was concerned to do something as quickly as possible to help Gaius who, regrettably, had been thrown out of his church. Notice that John does not simply let the matter drop, as if it were a tragedy that nothing could be done about. He lets Gaius know of his intention to come and deal definitively with the problem. So, in effect, he says, "Gaius, you did all the right things. Keep on doing them. But sit tight and don't attempt to do anything more about the problem with Diotrephes; help is coming as soon as possible." John does not hope that the problem will go away. Nor does he think that it is irremediable. And he doesn't tell Gaius to try to start another church since this one is obviously "down the tubes." No. Though, for a time, Gaius might have to make do with the few others who like him had been thrown out of the church (notice the plural in v. 10), John will so discipline Diotrephes, and any others who were siding with him, that the church will be rid of him once and for all. John is coming to preserve the congregation, not to give up on it. All of this is in the background of what he wrote. There is more, but we shall take it up in other chapters.

The idea of using other means of counseling apart from face-to-face sessions is certainly biblical. But clearly, it is only a substitute for the face-to-face encounter. John intimates as much when he writes that he will soon come and *then*, as he longed to do, he would speak to Gaius face to face (literally, in Greek, "mouth to mouth"). In verses 13 and 14 John says that he doesn't want to write more, doubtless because under the circumstances, it was so inadequate. Indeed, most counselors would agree that there is no final substitute for the personal counseling session, even though at times it may be necessary to use other means.[1]

---

1. As to the relative effectiveness of mail over other forms of counseling, there is some question. Paul, we saw, used the longer letter to counsel effectively. John, writing to Gaius, was effective. In more recent times, Phillips and Wiener (*Short Term Psychotherapy and Structured Behavior Change*) did counseling by letter in which they report that it was every bit as effective as the personal, face-to-face interview. But once they used non-Christian principles of counseling their evaluation of the results is quite problematic. So far as I know, there is no other study of the subject.

Chapter Four
Church Discipline: Used and Misused

The tendency to misuse the power of church discipline is great. Diotrephes' actions provide the earliest recorded instance of the misuse of church discipline. Sadly, it was not the last. The history of the church is replete with many examples of its misuse. That is one reason why, in modern times, church discipline has all but disappeared from American churches.[1] Overuse and misuse combine to make the churches shy away from church discipline. Yet we may not do so. The answer is not to neglect or abandon discipline but to use it correctly – that is, biblically.[2]

What, in essence, was wrong about Diotrephes' use of discipline? At the core of what he did was the use of church discipline for *his own personal advantage*. He didn't care a pin for the brothers, nor for the members of his flock who were following the best apostolic traditions. He cared only about himself. That is the most heinous misuse of discipline possible. One may misuse discipline out of ignorance or from misunderstanding of the biblical passages involved. That is bad enough. But to willfully determine to achieve one's own selfish ends by its use, rather than the clear biblical ends God has set forth, is far worse.

John identifies the problem: Diotrephes "loves the place of preeminence" (v. 9). Self-aggrandizement was what motivated him! The seriousness of the problem may be seen not only from what John determines to do about it, but also from verse 11, where John intimates that

---

1. A few generations past saw an overuse of church discipline. Often, it was used for the wrong reasons – notably, to get rid of troublemakers (in such cases, it has been called "a back door revival"). Of course, that is a quite wrong use of church discipline; instead, the repentance and restoration of the wrongdoer should always be a prime goal. Yet, in time, its misuse eventuated in its lack of use and eventual disuse.

2. For details on how to do so, see my book *The Handbook of Church Discipline*.

Diotrephes' actions may indicate that his profession of faith was false ("the one who does evil hasn't seen God"[1]).

The problem that often occurs for a counselor or counselee today, where church discipline has been reinstituted, is that it has been misused. It may be necessary for a counselor to be faced with determining whether or not a given church has exercised discipline properly in accordance with the Scriptures. As in this letter, the crux of the counseling problem may lie right there. Until the truth or falsity of a counselee's claim in this regard is determined, it may not be possible to make headway in counseling.

In all such cases (it is particularly difficult when the counselee is disciplined by one church and then applies for membership in the counseling pastor's own church), the counselor must get to the bottom of the matter. He must listen to the counselee's description of what happened, but he may not settle for that (cf. Proverbs 18:17). There are always at least three sides to any issue. There are the parties who are at odds, and there is God.

When considering the matter, the counselor must know the facts. That means he will contact the pastor of the disciplining church (letting the counselee know that he must do so) to learn their view of things. Then, with the biblical materials spread plainly before him, he must evaluate what he has learned from both parties. He may find it necessary to bring them all together. God's way, it sometimes turns out, is different from that of both parties to the dispute. At other times, he will clearly see how either the counselee or the disciplining church has erred. Unless the wrong use of discipline was due to personal advantage (as in the case of Diotrephes) or some other entirely unbiblical motive, he will attempt to bring order out of chaos by gently, but clearly, setting forth what the Bible says to all of those concerned.

---

1. In this verse John seems to be contrasting Demetrius with Diotrephes.

If the disciplining pastor and his church are of a willing mind when it comes to following the Bible, they will acknowledge and right the wrong. That may lead to reconciliation between the counselee and the church from which he was dismissed. On the other hand, the counselee may have been wrong and the church right. Again, if the counselee's heart is right, he will accept this and right all wrongs; then reconciliation may proceed.

But matters do not always take those turns. Either the church or pastor may receive correction poorly, revealing a heart filled with pride, or the counselee may act stubbornly as well (or both may happen). In such cases, the matter must often be adjudicated at higher levels of the denomination to which the church belongs. Or the ejection of the counselee by the church may have to be sustained by all concerned. In the case of independent congregations, where there is no higher level to turn to, the matter becomes complex. Others, if possible, may need to be called in to judge the matter. Clearly John, himself, as an apostle, was the "higher level."

At this higher level, John asserts his apostolic authority that Diotrephes not only refused to "recognize" (v. 9) but also abused (v. 10). There is authority in the church, although from the way in which some preachers preach and act you'd hardly know so. Jesus Christ stands behind the proper discipline of the church and He works through it: "Where two or three meet together in My Name, I am there among them" (Matthew 18:20). This verse has nothing to do with small prayer meetings. It comes at the conclusion of the fundamental passage on church discipline (Matthew 18:15–20). It is the Lord's assurance that He is there as the process takes place, lending all of His authority to what is being done by the elders of the church "gathered together" to exercise discipline. It is sad when discipline is removed from a church; much of Christ's authority disappears along with it.

John says, "when I come, I shall remember everything

21

that he has done." He does not mean merely that he will be careful not to forget anything. Of course, that is true; but he will not allow *anything* to be swept under the carpet. He is not speaking primarily of remembering in contrast to forgetting. In the Bible, "to remember" also means "to deal summarily with" someone.[1] John is saying something like this: "Diotrephes may not recognize my authority now, but when I come he will recognize it – or else!" John, of course, had apostolic authority, which might have meant he would use miraculous power similar to that which the apostles sometimes exerted against evil persons, as we see in the book of Acts. John, the apostle of love, was also the "son of thunder." Love for the church and its members often will lead to thunderous responses on the part of God's ministers. But without the miraculous element, you must recognize that your authority as a minister of the Word is no less than John's when you act in accordance with the Bible. Like John, you must be willing to assert it whenever it is necessary – even if it means going toe to toe with another minister who, like Diotrephes, has been sinning and will not repent.

The act of Diotrephes was schism. He separated members of the church for invalid reasons. God's clear teaching on schism is found in Titus 3:10 where Paul writes, "After counseling him once or twice, give up on a divisive person, and have nothing more to do with him." That is a decisive word. Paul is saying don't continue to work with him, as (presumably) you would with persons who have lesser problems. When someone is splitting the church, and he fails to respond to proper counsel, then write him off. Don't continue to counsel him. Why such haste? The answer is clear: he is *divisive*. That is to say, by what he is doing or saying, he is dividing the church. That usually happens when someone seeks to "drag away disciples to follow"

---

1. See also I Samuel 15:2, 3. In Jeremiah 31:34 God says, "I will remember their sin no more." By that He means He will not punish them for it. God never *forgets* anything.

him (Acts 20:30). That sort of person is anxious to proselytize among the brothers of the church. Seventh Day Adventists, Jehovah's Witnesses, and Mormons are notorious for doing this. But it may happen among those who adhere to true doctrines. Someone, for his own pernicious reasons, attempts to split the church. As in the case of Diotrephes, when this happens, it is usually because of personal ambition. Paul's words indicate that if something is not done immediately, the schismatic person may go on with his nefarious actions and truly divide the congregation. If he doesn't listen to initial counsel, then, as soon as possible, take action to deal with him. John had written something to the church to no avail. After this one exhortation, he was through reasoning with Diotrephes who had already split the church. He was going to "have nothing more to do with him" by way of counseling him as a brother. In cases of schism, swift action is required. Tragically, such action is seldom taken soon enough.

However in III John, the problem is not one of "dragging" disciples away from the church; rather it is a matter of splitting the church by driving people out (presumably through church discipline wrongly exercised). Schism, then, can come from the outside or from within. Either way, it must be treated as a heinous sin. It cannot be countenanced under any circumstances.

Chapter Five
Attacking the Counselor

While the attack was verbal, Diotrephes' words were vicious enough to make one think that if John had been in the vicinity, he might have been manhandled. Listen again to what John writes:

I have written something to the church, but Diotrephes, who loves the place of preeminence among them, doesn't recognize our authority. For that reason, when I come, I shall remember everything that he has done; for example, the evil words that he babbles about us! And as though that were not enough, he himself doesn't recognize the authority of the brothers, but stops those who wants to, and throws them out of the church (III John 9, 10).

Diotrephes, of course, never agreed to counsel with John. In fact, he refused even to listen to his authoritative, apostolic words. In the strict sense of the term, he was not a counselee. But John treated him as such, seeking to direct him to handle matters at the church properly. That's why John wrote to the church and to him.

Presumably, the conflict arose over whether hospitality should be granted to the visiting brothers who (as all missionaries did in those days[1]) sought to stay at the homes of Christians as they traveled. These Christians would put them up for a while, then give them adequate provisions to travel to the home of a Christian in the next town. But while

---

1. In the *didache* (*The Teaching of the Twelve Apostles*) 13:2, we read, "If indeed he that comes is a wayfarer help him as much as you can, but he shall not remain with you longer than two or three days, unless there be a necessity." Directions for receiving and treating apostles and prophets are also given (11:3–12). Hospitality was an important matter. Teaching elders were required to be hospitable as one of their qualifications for office (Titus 1:8). Clearly, by his lack of hospitality, Diotrephes disqualified himself from the office.

staying with the Christian, doubtless they would often be asked to speak to the congregation, telling them of the Lord's goodness and the things that He had done through their missionary endeavors. It was this to which Diotrephes objected so strenuously. He would not have these missionaries in his pulpit, getting all the admiration and glory rather than himself! So in order to stop the practice, he forbade any member of the congregation to receive the missionaries. In that way, they would not be able to influence any of his church members or stay long enough to speak. They would be forced to move on to the next place – presumably suffering hardship as a result.

Now there were some who knew that this directive went counter to the teaching of John and other apostles and the spirit of loving fellowship that ought to exist among brothers in Christ. So they disobeyed Diotrephes' directive and took in the missionaries so they would not have to suffer because of this unchristian directive! When Diotrephes realized that they had flaunted his authority (which he was misusing), he was angry and threw these Christians out of the church.[1]

John heard about the action of Diotrephes and wrote to the church about it. If Diotrephes was the pastor, as we must presume him to be because of the power he was able to exert against those who disobeyed him, the letter probably would be sent to the church through him. At any rate, he read it, became furious at John, and began to slander him before everyone. The terms that John uses are expressive:

1. "evil words" (*ponerois,* using malicious speech, making false charges)

2. "he babbles about us" (*phluaron,* chattering about; the idea being that of making foolish, nonsensical, or groundless accusations)

---

1. The word is a strong one: *ekballo,* literally, "to throw out."

John clearly describes an unreasonable response on the part of Diotrephes that grew out of anger. In short, Diotrephes *attacked* John as a person.

Now, whenever a counselee fails to achieve the goals that he has in mind (even if they are not God's goals) and, particularly, if his pride is challenged in one way or another, it is quite possible that he will launch an attack upon the counselor. He may spread false accusations, claim all sorts of nonsensical things about him, and maliciously seek to drag him down in the eyes of others.

Counselors must quite frequently point out a counselee's sin. Often, confronting that sin involves dealing with the counselee's pride and evil ambition. Many counselees rebel at this. Someone who has wronged another, for instance, may be willing to admit the fact to his counselor. But when he is told that he must not only confess the sin to God, but also to the one he has wronged, he digs in his heels. That would be embarrassing. No, he "cannot" do that! Such embarrassment grows out of a high estimate of himself. Until he is willing to lower that estimate, his repentance is in doubt. Diotrephes, who wanted the preeminence and would not share the limelight with the missionaries, was greatly angered when John took him to task for his sin. To deal properly with it, Diotrephes would have had to admit his wrongdoing *and* to change his ways. He was not about to do that before those around him. So he thought the way to eliminate the pressure was to attack John.

When a counselee attacks you as a counselor, how do you respond? Well, what did John do? He stuck to his guns! He wrote Gaius, describing how he saw the situation, telling him what was the problem with Diotrephes, and informing him that he would soon come to set things right. He also sent Demetrius, who probably carried the letter, to do what he could until John came.

In this, you see that John did not run away from the problem; he met it head on. That is how a counselor ought to deal with attacks on himself. The point here is not that one must defend himself (John was not interested in that) but that Christ was being dishonored and members of the flock were being hurt and scattered. That cannot be allowed. As a counselor who counsels in the Name of Jesus Christ from His Word, you may not allow counselees to defame that counseling. You, too, must meet it head on. You must expose the lies of the Diotrephes who attacks you and tell the truth[1] to those who have been told falsehoods about you or about biblical counseling. Too many counselors back off when attacked. That was not John's way.[2]

If you are a counselee, you should take warning from this letter and reign in your anger. Learn to control your tongue. It is easy to lash out verbally against a counselor who has attempted to help you and the church when he finds it necessary to expose your sin in some way that "steps on your pride." Read James 1:26; 3:1–12 over and over prayerfully if you find it difficult to "tame" your tongue. You can't; but God can enable you to do so.

---

1. Notice John's concern for truth in this letter. Five times in this brief epistle the word appears. Love is not true love unless it is "in the truth" (v. 1). The loving thing to do is to respond to an attack God's way – as John did. See my book *Maintaining the Delicate Balance* for more on "love in the truth."

2. Or Paul's. The entire letter of II Corinthians is a defense against malicious attacks.

Chapter Six
Taking Sides

The message of the book of III John may be divided into two parts: Diotrephes is wrong, Gaius is right. There is no doubt about which side John finds himself on. He "took sides" with Gaius, the brothers, and others who may have been put out of the church, against Diotrephes.

Most counselors find it difficult to "take sides." Many will avoid doing so at all costs. And there is good reason for this extreme hesitancy – the situation may not be as clear as it was in the problem that John addressed. Sometimes, there is fault on both sides of an issue. In such circumstances, it is wise not to side with one or the other party in a counseling case. Nevertheless, there are times when siding with one party against another is called for, is inevitable, and can't be avoided. The case against Diotrephes and for Gaius was one of these.

As much as you may not like to "take sides," you must break through your natural hesitancy if God's Word, God's Name, or God's people are in jeopardy. How may you do this without alienating people? How can you help but pitting one person against another? In such cases what you ought to think is not, "I am taking sides with one or more of the persons involved," but, rather, "I am taking God's side!"

Once a man called me about the possibility of getting counseling for himself and his wife. In the course of the phone call, he said: "My Christian doctor sides with me and my pastor sides with my wife. I'm afraid that it won't be long before you side with one or the other of us and we will reach an impasse – then the other person will no longer listen to what you have to say. It always works out that way."

In response, I said, "Well, I don't plan to side with either of you. I plan to side with God!"

He then said, "That sounds different," and they came. In the course of counseling, I found that siding with God meant that with respect to some issues I was on the husband's side and with respect to others, on his wife's.[1] But always, in the discussion I kept on asking, "Now here is what God says in His Word; who agrees with Him and who doesn't?"

By using that approach, which is quite biblical, I was able to avoid the charge of "siding" with one or the other. And of course, that is exactly what a counselor should do, and it is exactly what a counselee should wish him to do. To take sides, then, is to take God's side. In the situation involving Gaius and Diotrephes, Gaius was on God's side and Diotrephes was not. That is the point.

There is never a time when a counselor may allow himself to side with anyone other than God. He must remember that He represents God when he calls his counseling "Christian" or "biblical." The "ministry of the Word" is *God's* ministry of *God's* Word. If it is going to be so, then the counselor must use the Scriptures as his standard, allowing God to determine what the counselees involved must believe and do. When he does, he will find himself siding with a counselee when that counselee believes and acts in accordance with the Bible.

On the other hand, there may be times when he must stand alone with God against everything that counselees believe or do concerning some issue. Both counselees may have an unbiblical view of things. On such occasions, there is no need to lean toward one or the other. Now, I did not say that everyone will be happy when you "take God's side." What many want you to do is to side with *them*. But you must continue to respond biblically. Someone says, "But don't you think I'm right?" (trying to get you on his/her side of an issue). You respond, "I'm not so much concerned about whether or not I agree with you; my concern

---

1. Or to put it more accurately, on some issues the husband was on God's side and on others the wife was. On other issues both were not on God's side.

is about what God thinks. Let's turn to the Scriptures and see what He says about the matter."

Three great verses to bring into the discussion at the proper time are Isaiah 55:7, 8, 11, where God is speaking about repentance for *our* ways and *our* thoughts which are not right because they are not like *His* ways and *His* thoughts. There He says we must "forsake" our ways and thoughts, "return" to Him [i.e., repent], and start thinking as He does and walking in His paths. And the way in which this may be done is by taking heed to God's "Word" which does not go forth in vain, but accomplishes the purposes for which it was written (v. 11).

Now, notice the comparison in the verses mentioned above. It is between our thoughts and ways and God's as found in His Word. The average counselee who is in conflict with another has it wrong. He is making comparisons between himself and another person. Or he may want to compare his ideas with those of the counselor. The right approach is to bring counselees to a place where they compare their thoughts and their ways with God's – not with anyone else's. Paul tellingly made this point in Galatians 6:4:

> But let each one test his own work; then he will have something to boast about in himself alone, rather than comparing himself with another.

The "test" of course, is precisely what I have been saying – one must compare his thoughts and his ways with God's as they are found in His Word.

As I said, you will not always be popular with counselees when you take God's side. But one thing is plain – if you are clear about what you are doing, no one may ever rightly accuse you of siding with someone else. He may disagree with your interpretation or with your application of the Bible, but he will be able to see plainly where you are coming from. So counselor, always bring God and His Word into the picture. After all, what makes biblical counseling "biblical"?

31

Chapter Seven
Counseling "Gaiuses"

Plainly, the attempt to counsel Diotrephes failed to produce the desired results. In God's providence, however, what *He* desired *did* take place. Often there is unexpected[1] fallout from "failure." One of those unexpected items was the opportunity to counsel Gaius in the midst of a crisis. And as a result of that opportunity, which John seized upon, Gaius was greatly assured and strengthened in his faith and we, today, have the matchless gem that we call III John!

The opposition of Diotrephes to the righteous acts of Gaius and his fellows who were also ousted from the church, occasioned John to write to Gaius. In this letter, three things stand out:

1. John's *praise* of Gaius

2. John's *assurance* that Gaius had done the right thing

3. John's *encouragement* of Gaius

Let's consider each of these items.

John has high praise for Gaius – not only for what Gaius had done in the face of opposition from Diotrephes but also for Gaius' lifestyle ("walk") in general. The brothers had returned to John telling him of how Gaius was "walking in the truth." John expresses great joy ("no greater joy") and gratitude that one whom he had led to faith in Christ was walking in the truth. He even tells Gaius that such a testimony brings him immense joy. In the salutation, he refers to Gaius as prospering spiritually even more than he was prospering physically or financially.[2] John was lavish in his praise of Gaius, but the praise was well-deserved. The report from the brothers was unmistakable, and John

---

1. That is, unexpected to us; not to God who providentially arranges such things.

2. The use of this twist in the common greeting used in letters in John's day is one reason for thinking that John took some pains about writing this letter.

believed it to be true.

You can imagine after all the controversy that Gaius had been through how welcome these words of praise must have been! If Diotrephes would speak as he did about an apostle (v. 10), think how violent and insulting his words must have been toward Gaius and others who opposed him! John was not "buttering" Gaius up. He was expressing an honest opinion. In the face of great difficulty, Gaius had acted faithfully according to the "truth" that John had taught him. To a defeated, discouraged, and possibly con-fused believer, his words must have been like a drink of cold water on a scorching hot day.

In counseling others who have faced problems success-fully, but have been defeated by those who oppose, it is always wise to find something in what they have done that you can *honestly* commend them for. Notice the italics in the last sentence; they are of importance. If for nothing else, you can always praise counselees for being true to the Lord. To praise someone, however, you must always be careful not to stretch the truth or to allow the praise of a man to overshadow the fact that it was God who made all of this possible. John's emphasis upon the "truth," which he mentions five times in this letter, makes God's side in this very clear. It is because Gaius has been instructed in the *truth from God* that he knew what to do and did it. Knowing the truth not only guided him in his actions, but also strengthened him in his resolution to stand in opposi-tion to Diotrephes. He believed the truth and acted accord-ingly. Strictly speaking, praise is not counsel, yet it certainly creates the right atmosphere for it.[1]

The second bit of counsel (here actual counseling begins) has to do with *assuring* Gaius. Gaius had taken radi-cal action: he had disobeyed the pastor of his church. That is not something that is to be recommended or done

---

1. Notice in the letters to the churches in the book of Revelation, how the Lord first commends what can honestly be commended about each church.

lightly. Indeed, it should not be done except under the most extreme circumstances and for reasons that are clearly in accord with "the truth." The consistent teaching of the apostles was "Obey your leaders and submit to them" (Hebrews 13:17). Under ordinary circumstances, no support should be given to those who violate that injunction. In most cases where such disobedience has taken place the counselor must stand against it. However, disobedience was warranted in this situation. So John *assures* Gaius that what he did, he did "faithfully." That is, it was in accordance with those things that he had been taught. Hospitality was always to be extended to true teachers of the Word; indeed, as we saw, such hospitality was enjoined upon elders in the church.

Assurance from counselors who, like John, proclaim God's Word in such volatile situations is important. The tendency of one who is anxious to please the Lord is to hold off, to be very sure that what he is doing is right. He knows he should obey the elders of the church and that to disobey could be a very great sin. So for a tender believer to do as Gaius did is very difficult. But he went ahead courageously doing what he thought was right according to the truth. Then John came along and assured him that his response was correct, that it accords with the faith.

When you assure someone that some radical action he has taken is right – even though down inside he may have some doubts – you must be sure it is well-founded biblically. Otherwise, as a counselor, you could be an accessory to sin after the fact! You must always, therefore, be able to support such assurance by clear biblical teaching. Nothing less than that will do.

You must also realize that in a world of sin, in which persons who are far from completely sanctified hold places of power in the church, there will be more than one Diotrephes to contend with. There are times, therefore, in which you must assure counselees that disobedience is proper. To assure someone who has faced up to the sinful actions of another, who with difficulty has responded to it in righteous ways that some might question, that his response was "faithful" (according to the faith), is often necessary. It can be the very best counsel that you can offer, however, it takes certainty (and often courage).

You may be faced with a situation in which a counselee has left a church because the pastor and the elders refuse to support biblical counseling and, in the face of plenty of information to the contrary, insist on referring their members to a non-christian psychiatrist who has already messed up the lives of a number of persons.[1] The Scripture is plain: if a person is caught in sin, he is to be restored by those "who have the Spirit" (Galatians 6:1); not by unbelievers who do not have the Spirit. This makes offering assurance doubly difficult, since you too are a counselor and, as a result, you may be attacked for merely pitting your own counseling views against another's. It is easy for those who oppose you to level false charges in such a situation. Yet believing that the move is right before God, you must stick to your guns and assure your counselee that his action was correct.

The third way in which John counseled Gaius was to encourage him to go on doing the very thing that led to his expulsion from the church. He told him that he would "do well" to continue offering hospitality whenever missionaries came through his community (III John 6). Furthermore, John even instructed him about how to do so (III John 6,7), and laid it upon him as an obligation (III John 8).

Take the modern example I mentioned a couple of paragraphs above. Not only should you assure the person who is leaving the church that fails to minister to its members scripturally that he is right in doing so, you should help him make the move. This may involve directing him to come to your own church – a fact that opens you to the charge of sheep stealing. Under ordinary circumstances, if his pastor

---

1. One of whom may have been his wife.

and elders were true shepherds, you would encourage him to return and straighten out any matters that were causing him to think of leaving. But, presumably, that would not be considered by those who would attack you, and you might even be slandered for encouraging him to move to your church! Nevertheless, that sort of *encouragement* is precisely what the counselee needs under the circumstances.

In all of this, it is important to see that counseling in the face of failure may open up other counseling opportunities. Someone has said that "it is an ill wind that brings no good." That is precisely the point. God always has some good to bring out of the sin man commits.[1] As a counselor who looks for it, you can do much good to help counselees who, apart from your counsel, might see only the problem itself.

---

1. For more on this see my book, *How to Handle Trouble.*

Chapter Eight
Helping Gaiuses to Recoup

My dictionary says that "to recoup" is "to make up for." In the biblical sense, it is to bring good out of evil, to find God's good in the problem. First, as a background to recouping, notice that John's letter to Gaius holds out *hope*. It may be a while – not long – but a while, and he will come and set everything in order. He will "remember" all that Diotrephes has done, and he will deal with him appropriately! Then (it is assumed) he will bring about a change in the situation in Gaius' church. People who may have supported Diotrephes in his iniquity will also either repent or, they too will be dealt with. "Big John is a'comin'!" All is not lost. In time, all will work out for God's honor and the church's good. "Gaius, keep your hopes alive!"

Giving hope is essential in crises like this one. A person who stood for the truth against opposition, and seemingly has lost, needs to know not only that he is right, but that others true to the faith stand with him. I cannot tell you how many times a biblical counselor has said something like the following to me: "It's so good to be here at this meeting where there are so many others who are like-minded. I thought I was about the only one!" There are always the 7000 who have not bowed the knee to Baal. And if you continue the conversation with that lonely counselor for very long, you will frequently hear stories about how he was persecuted because of his stand for the truth. Of course, sometimes it isn't persecution; sometimes by his crude and even belligerent attitude he has brought it all on himself. But more often, the person is denigrated because of outright opposition to doing things biblically and sometimes may be driven from a church. His words indicate how welcome companionship in biblical beliefs and practices can be. So never think that a word of hope, a word that indicates the persecuted person isn't alone, a word that someone is willing to stand with and help in spite of opposition is unimportant.

Moreover, point out the assets that one still possesses. John stresses in this case that Gaius isn't alone. Others have been ejected from the church along with him (notice the word "them" in v. 10) and these "friends" are still in fellowship with Gaius (v. 14). If the data indicate that there are others who also have experienced "failure" along with your counselee, point out that he is not alone. Moreover, even if one has been disfellowshipped wrongly, you may tell him that *in God's sight* he is still a member of the church. That's what verse 14 plainly implies. In that verse, John includes both Gaius and his friends as still belonging to the body of Christ. They are to be greeted by him in John's name, and the church where John recognized them as fellow believers. Verse 14 contains language that appertains to the fellowship of the *saints*. In spite of what happened, John does not consider Gaius and his friends anything less than members in good standing of the church of Christ. That he has not broken fellowship with them should greatly encourage Gaius and his friends. It is important not only for you, but also for your congregation to stand with such persons in their extremities and to recognize their proper status as saints.

Making decisions like this, in which you must side with people whom others have wrongly rejected is never easy. But sometimes it is necessary. One caution – always be sure that you have all the necessary facts to make a judgment like this. John demonstrates that he does (v. 9, 10). Obviously, he had two or three reliable witnesses in the missionary brothers who had fully informed him of the situation. Perhaps, there were even more. It is wise to make such judgments only in the company of others – namely, the elders of your church. John was an apostle; you are not!

Gaius could also be glad that the problem with Diotrephes clarified matters that might have been hazy before. There are few things as useful to bring truth to its full brilliance as to have to understand how it relates to a crisis. Sincere study of the Word of God at such a time (not study to bolster a viewpoint by finding what one *wants* to find by twisting the Scriptures) will become most profitable. Once I preached on John 1 and, in passing, happened to mention the Jehovah's Witnesses' wrong understanding of the first verse and how to counter it. The next day I got a phone call from a member asking how to respond to a Jehovah's Witness about John 1:1. I asked, "Weren't you there in church yesterday when I mentioned this very thing?" She said, "Yes, but this morning a Jehovah's Witness came to the door!" When one finds it necessary to *use* the Bible in actual life situations, he may be much more motivated to dig until he finds truth.

Trials also have a way of raising issues that, otherwise, might lie dormant. Not only did all sorts of matters about church discipline arise in Gaius' confrontation of Diotrephes, but all sorts of matters concerning the reception and support of missionaries came to light. The fact that Christians should support missionaries "in a manner that is worthy of God" (v. 6) is an important insight. I have been told that missionaries have received used tea bags and used razor blades and worn carpets that no one would even think of leaving on his own floor. That is hardly the way to treat them. Rather, the important word in verse 6 suggests that whatever we do for missionaries ought to be done in the very best way. They should be treated as one would treat God Himself! If this controversy had not brought this important insight to light, we would not have it since you cannot find it elsewhere in the Bible.

In addition, there is the further insight that the missionaries refused to take any support from the heathen to whom they preached (v. 7). This very important principle, that believers alone should support the work of the church, has often been violated by the church. But would we know about it if, in God's providence, Diotrephes had not done as he did?

And, don't miss the fact that God considers those who

properly support missions "fellow workers for the truth" (v. 8). This simple but profound statement is one of the most powerful incentives for missionary support in the Scriptures. Yet apart from the difficulties that were experienced by Gaius and his friends, would it have surfaced?

So you get the point, don't you? Trials bring forth information that might otherwise not have appeared. We may rejoice, then, that in recouping (making up for what has been lost) we receive something as valuable – or more so! This is a crucial point to raise with counselees. Indeed, a counselor who is adept at observing such things will help many more than the one who is not.

We may also learn how to avoid similar failures in the future. The problem with Diotrephes stemmed from ungodly ambition in his heart. John says so: Diotrephes "loved" the "place of preeminence" (v. 9). Self-centered pride occasioned all of this. How utterly important it is to ask the Spirit to use His Word to crush all personal pride and ambition in ourselves! But would the problem (there is a little of Diotrephes in the best of us, isn't there?) ever have been etched out as clearly had the difficulty with Diotrephes not arisen? Again, in recouping from "failure," we can avoid making a disastrous turn in the road that would hinder "successful" Christian living – that is, living that pleases God.

Recouping, then, is something that any faithful counselor may help a counselee do. It is not some makeshift way of coping with failure. No. Exactly not that! Rather, it is a way of unearthing all that God has provided for us in His providence in the experience that He has planned and has effected. To fail to recoup is to fail to benefit from failure. It is a second failure, this one on the part of the one who may have been wronged. To recoup is to learn and to gain all that one can from the experience. If his attitude is right, then one will look for the gains that he can make in his Christian life. Good counselors do not merely empathize with the counselee; they help him to recoup so as to glean the most that God has for him in his failures.

Chapter Nine
Bringing Success Out of Failure

We have already discussed several ways to bring success out of failure by approaching the problem in a biblical attitude, searching out those things that we can learn from it, and acting in the situation as God would have us to act. This last factor needs a bit more explication.

We know that when he arrived, as he expected to do soon (v. 14), John would have taken summary action to rectify matters at the church of which Diotrephes was the pastor. But we do not have an account of what that action would have been. Let us, then, consider what he would have done. How can we know? Well, we cannot know everything, of course, but by consulting other biblical passages we may surmise rather closely what sorts of things would have happened.

In a previous chapter, we referred to Titus 3:10, where Paul tells us that after one or two nouthetic confrontations we are to give up on a divisive person. The word translated "give up" is *paraiteomai*. This word might be translated many ways, such as "turn away from, beg off from, avoid." The idea behind the term is "to have nothing to do with." John, consequently, would have already determined that Diotrephes was to be handed over to Satan.[1] In his own mind, he would have informally disfellowshipped and defrocked him (cf. I Corinthians 5:3–5). When he arrived, doubtless, he would have made a similar, formal declaration of this decision to the church. Depending on how the congregation received his apostolic sentence, John would respond accordingly. If Diotrephes had so won over the portion of the congregation that remained and supported him, John would have urged them to repent and turn him out of their pulpit. If only a small number of them

---

1. See my book *The Handbook of Church Discipline* for details concerning church discipline.

responded positively to John's plea and, consequently, were also thrown out, John might have found it necessary to declare the church "Ichabod" ("the glory has departed") and organize a new congregation.

But probably, since he carried such weight as an apostle, he would have been able to reach the majority of the congregation who would have responded positively to his call to repentance and to ridding themselves of a "minister" who did not minister to them as he should. In such a case, he would have had a lot of work to do with individuals who had become separated over the Diotrephes affair. Hard words are usually spoken during such dust ups that need to be dealt with in terms of confession of sin and forgiveness. Reconciliation of members who had become estranged, falsehoods that were implanted in the minds of some by Diotrephes, and many other interpersonal stresses and strains would have to be worked through. It would not be a simple matter of getting rid of Diotrephes. In fact, getting rid of Diotrephes – apart from the use of miraculous power – might have been impossible. He had already shown his violent temper and vicious response to what, surely, was a reasonable, mild initial letter of exhortation from John. How would he take being ousted? Unless repentant, he would act more viciously – perhaps violently. It might be necessary to take physical measures to restrain him.

At any rate, John's first concern would have been to save the church, or as many of the members of it as possible. Having done that and having disposed of Diotrephes, as I said, his work would have only begun. Probably, he would have taken over the pulpit himself for a time as well as met in counseling sessions with most, if not all, of the persons involved in the problem. This would have taken much time and effort.

Now, I have set the matter up as if we were watching John at work. The fact is, there is much in this for the counselor today. If he is able to bring order out of chaos in a situation involving church discipline, and perhaps even involving the dismissal of a pastor from his charge (possibly through denominational or congregational action), he has only begun the work that must be done. The reconciliation process between those who opposed one another is most important, but time consuming.

If he is unable to successfully achieve the dismissal of the erring pastor and must form another congregation, he must always be sure that he works through the established denominational agencies or some other authoritative body. Rarely, but it might occur, he may find himself in the position of either bringing a large number of people into his own congregation or helping them to form a new one. This is not easy for a busy counselor to do, especially while receiving flak. But in this book I am not dealing with easily-handled matters. I'm dealing with the "messy stuff" that few persons wish to handle. Counselors, because of the matters in which they are involved, will find themselves, sooner or later, knee deep in the messy stuff. The problem is – how many counselors are prepared for that? How many would allow themselves to become involved? How many, if they did become involved, would know what to do? The time to think these things over is *before* they take place. Unlike the woman who didn't listen until the Jehovah's Witness rang her doorbell, a counselor ought always to be preparing himself for the unlikely. He never knows beforehand when it will occur!

Most cases will not be so sticky, but every one that concerns the division of a congregation, dissension from the pastoral ministry, or difficulty with troublemakers who want to disturb the peace of the church usually ends up in someone failing. It is then that the principles that we have discussed, which help those who want to do God's will in spite of the "failure" that occurred, come into play.

This book is not intended to discourage the counselor, but to prepare him, as much as possible, to meet cases that *are* sticky. Other books that I have written do not get into these matters, but the principles that are taught in them (many of which I have not mentioned here) are applicable. Anyone who busies himself with matters like these will want to peruse the several books that teach general counseling principles[1] and my *Handbook of Church Discipline*.

This chapter will be one to which you may have to refer from time to time. If you find that you are getting in over your head, please contact a more experienced biblical counselor for help. Be sure that you work within the denominational framework so long as that framework is scriptural. Have a group of elders solidly behind your moves whenever you deal with another congregation or any of its members. In all things, reach first for the simple biblical solution, as John did; become more complex only when driven to do so – as John was. In all things be wise as serpents, harmless as doves!

---

1. Such as the sections in *Competent to Counsel, How to Help People Change, The Christian Counselor's Manual* on reconciliation, and especially, *From Forgiven to Forgiving*.

Chapter Ten
The Person and the Issue

One problem is that some counselors are issue-oriented. But if the relationship of individuals to one another is not properly dealt with, all the right answers to issues usually will be of little help. If, for instance, a husband and wife are at odds, you can explain to them precisely how to solve some simple problem in their marriage, but they will not do so. They will find excuses, make objections, or do anything else rather than adopt and follow the proposed solution. So, you must spend time working on their relationship before you can help them solve their problems.

Now John must have recognized this fact. Here is a church torn apart by its wicked pastor who threw people out of its midst for doing good. But what, in this brief letter of only 14 verses does he concentrate on? The issue? Hardly. Out of the 14 verses only two are devoted to the issue itself (v. 9, 10). The other twelve concern people and their lives.

Here is something that we, as counselors ought to give heed to. We may tend to get so wrapped up in the issue that we almost forget the people involved. That is clearly wrong. I have already mentioned how John encouraged and assured Gaius, praising him for his godly behavior and giving him hope. That is the sort of thing that goes a long way toward helping people decide to get involved in the solutions to their problems.

Suppose Gaius had become embittered at the treatment he endured at the hands of Diotrephes and decided to respond in kind. If Diotrephes had spread rumors about him, slandered him, and impugned his motives as he did to the apostle John, Gaius could very well have adopted a retaliatory response. The harsh response, however, as Proverbs tells us, is not the way that pleases God (Proverbs 15:1). Rather, He would have us respond in a softer way. Think of how much additional trouble Gaius could have caused with his tongue! He, and the others who were ejected from the church, could have drawn so sharp a line of division between themselves and those who remained in the congregation that John's task to bring about reconciliation would have been much more difficult. Moreover, Gaius would have disappointed his Lord and given Diotrephes something legitimate to complain about.

Now John must have been aware of this possibility and the many other temptations to respond in sinful ways that would be mimicking Diotrephes ("giving him some of his own medicine" is how we speak of it today) when he wrote "Dear friend, don't imitate evil, but imitate good." He was concerned about the manner in which Gaius would relate to Diotrephes and any others who might have been opposed to him. They had failed miserably, but he would not like to see failure spread to Gaius and his friends as well. So far, Gaius had shown admirable behavior. But under pressure, it is possible for that to deteriorate in time. John was quite aware of this and attempted to stay any yielding to the temptation.

Now, counselor and counselee, learn this: one seventh of the letter is devoted to the issue, six sevenths to the persons who must face it. Concern to approximate that proportion, at least in the initial stages as in this case, is what ought to drive everyone who is attempting to rectify matters. Until the hearts and actions of the persons who are a part of a dispute are right before God, and therefore before one another, there is little hope of a good outcome. In resolving problems, the attitudes of those involved are of great importance as I have mentioned in the example of the husband and wife. Yet how frequently do those who attempt to bring about solutions fail to realize this. Again, if that happens, we are confronted with an additional failure – handling the failure incorrectly. Instead of solutions, we encounter name calling, gossip, hard words, and hurt feelings. Until the counselor deals with these, it is unwise to attempt to take even preliminary steps toward a solution.

When relationships have been repaired, through elimination of troublemakers like Diotrephes and confession and forgiveness by all concerned, solutions (even to difficult problems) come quickly. Thus, rather than plunging into a tub of steaming hot water, first, draw some cold water to cool it down.

A temptation for biblical counselors is to adopt an abstract, academic approach that offers solutions – even biblical ones – but never to give heed to the relationship between the parties who are involved. But it is not the Bible's approach. Of course, God may bless His Word when it is offered even in this inadequate manner; that is His prerogative. He is often far better to us than we deserve! But just because He is merciful and good does not excuse us from doing the right thing. We should learn, therefore, from John's overwhelmingly personal approach how to deal with serious problems in the church. If we wish to recoup from failures we will not do it by failing in this regard. Further failure on our part will not bring good out of the failures of others. We must answer evil with good, not with evil (Romans 12:21[1]).

Notice how great an emphasis John places on Gaius' treatment of missionaries in the future. He is concerned that Gaius' good works in the past not be dulled by the sinful actions of Diotrephes. It is easy to come to the place where you say, "What's the use, anyway? I try to do the right thing and, first thing you know, this is what happens." You will hear that sort of thing all of the time. Meet it by strong encouragement to continue the good that one has done without discouragement. Indeed, John even lays out the highest way of doing so: treat the missionaries as if they were God Himself (v. 6). He even stresses the obligation by saying "We *ought* to..." (v. 8). Trouble is not to deter us from our obligations. The book of I Peter teaches

---

1. The entire twelfth chapter of Romans is pertinent to the question of counseling in the face of failure. See my exposition of this chapter (v. 14–21) in the book entitled *How to Overcome Evil*.

throughout that, in the face of all sorts of hardships, we must continue to trust and obey. Hardships do not relieve one from obeying God. Rather, they should only spur him on to greater obedience, knowing that in all problems God is working them together for one's good. If for nothing else, trials come in order to make us more like Christ (read Romans 8:29 along with 8:28!).

To minister to the person who is in a crisis situation, then, means to help him to maintain the right attitude, to call him to greater trust, and to urge him to higher obedience. In other words, you should be concerned to see him achieve a *personal* victory out of the failure. The situation may be beyond saving, but your counselee who has the Spirit dwelling within and the Word in his hand, is not.

Chapter Eleven
How Would You Counsel?

You have read and learned enough from the first ten chapters of this book to be able to apply some of what you have learned. So, I am suggesting that you try doing so right away. I am going to present a few scenarios for you to figure out. Sketch out your responses to each. If you do not know the answers, you may need to reread one or more chapters in this book or, possibly, some of the other books mentioned in the footnotes. As I said, the material dealt with here is "difficult stuff." Most of it is not for "beginners."[1] If you can deal with these examples successfully, you probably are an accomplished counselor – at least on paper (how you deal with people in person is a side we can only simulate to some extent here). If you are a "failure in this exercise," then at least try to figure out how to recoup.

1. In this scenario, everything else remains as it is in the book of III John. There is but one great difference: Gaius responds badly to what Diotrephes did. Instead of continuing to "walk in the truth," he goes off into a corner (not literally, of course) and begins to feel sorry for himself. He sulks, he whines, he is full of self-pity. If you were the apostle John, how would you write to Gaius in the letter? Demetrius has tried to help Gaius, but he won't listen. He calls on John to help since John led Gaius to faith in Christ.

2. In this second scenario, Gaius, not Diotrephes causes the problem. It is he that objects to receiving the mis-

---

1. It's true in my ministry, and others have told me that it is true in theirs also: God seems to have sent me the cases that I could handle at any given point in my development as a counselor. If I had had to tackle some of those that appeared later on at the beginning I wouldn't have had a clue. But whenever I felt myself getting a little overconfident, it seems that He also threw me a curve to baffle me and set me digging in the Bible for answers again. You will probably find the same true of your counseling ministry.

sionaries. "Missionaries, missionaries, missionaries!" he complains. "All we ever do in this church is listen to missionaries and entertain them. This wastes time and costs money! And – what's more – Diotrephes isn't doing his job as a pastor; he has missionaries in the pulpit instead of preparing sermons himself. I think we ought to reduce his salary. I'm tired of hearing missionary exploits instead of the Word of God!" Now there's a new twist for you. Supposing he wouldn't listen to Diotrephes or the elders of the church and, since you led Gaius to faith in Christ, they ask you (John) for help, what would you write?

3. In the third scenario we find the elders split over what to do about the behavior of Diotrephes. He refuses to receive the missionaries (as in the epistle), he is talking of throwing out those members who do so (in defiance of his directives to the contrary), but four out of his seven elders refuse to go along with this approach. The impasse comes to John's attention through a letter (confirmed by the missionary brothers) from Gaius. To whom will he write, and what will he say? To Diotrephes, to the elders, to Gaius or two all of the above?

4. In this fourth scenario, suppose that matters are as I sketched them in scenario 3, and John has written to Diotrephes (to no avail), as he did in III John, but he gets a call for help from one of the elders to whom he also has written. What will he write by way of response (he cannot yet travel to the church)?

5. In scenario five, everything is much the same as it is in the actual letter of III John except that some of Gaius' friends have left the church pronouncing "a pox on all churches!" John can't come to help at this point, Gaius doesn't know what to do (everything he has tried to do has failed) and he has appealed to John for help. John is familiar with the persons who have gone off in disgust,

but doesn't know them well. He will want to write to them and to Gaius. What will he write to each?

A. To Gaius
B. To Stephen (the leader of those who left in a huff)
C. To Mark (who went with Steve and Mark reluctantly)
D. To Andrew (who seems to be denying the faith altogether as a result of what Diotrephes did)

Chapter Twelve
Conclusion

In this book, I have spent time considering III John because it alone discusses the failure that involves missionaries, a pastor, his church, and members who have been ejected from it. It also treats many of the ways in which such circumstances must be handled. Matters in III John are, therefore, unique. Yet they mesh perfectly with principles inculcated elsewhere in the Scriptures. A thorough study of this brief, interesting epistle is mandatary for all biblical counselors if they want to be prepared to deal with the difficult cases.

I hope that the study will prove valuable not only to those who have been wrongly disciplined by churches that didn't know what they were doing – or didn't want to know – but also to those who seek to help them. Along the way, perhaps, some ancillary biblical principles not mentioned elsewhere may be learned. But above all, John's fascinating counseling letter shows what "love in the truth" (v. 1) is all about. Some have translated the verse "whom I love truly," but given the emphasis on truth in the rest of the letter, this seems an unlikely and misleading choice. What John is saying, in effect, is "I love you in the realm of the truth that we both hold in common, and because of that love I will not abandon you in your hour of need."

How he fulfills, and intends to fulfill that promise, is the subject of III John and the substance of what we have been studying. Counseling is more than giving advice (though that is an essential part of it). It is not only a matter of rebuke, exhortation, comfort, and giving encouragement and hope (though these are needed as well). It is also a matter of dealing with difficult matters involving pastors, elders, members, and denominations. That is where many counselors go wrong when they encounter these elements in their counseling. I hope that this book will not only open their eyes to what they might be getting into in certain instances, but that it will also enable them to safely thread their way through the minefields that they will find planted all about them. To counsel rightly often takes courage. It means that you may become ostracized, attacked, slandered, and the like. You cannot always win friends and influence people as you might like to. Counselors don't need to study Dale Carnegie; they need to study the apostle John!

While a great emphasis of John's first epistle is love, here that love is worked out as it combines with the "truth." As we see it in action and read it from the pen of the apostle, we see that love is not some sticky, sentimental thing. It can be hard in order to deal effectively with difficult matters in decisive ways. It does not shrink back. It does not pander to persons or show respect of persons. It does not abandon those who are in trouble because it would mean getting into trouble itself. It is persistent. It is biblical. It wields authority and it does so powerfully.

All the things that Paul said love is in I Corinthians 13 may be extrapolated to the things I have just mentioned, but it is left to the apostle John to show us how. In writing a letter in which he *shows* love *in the truth*, we see them come alive right before our eyes. Be grateful, counselor and counselee, for the small epistles of the New Testament written to meet situations in which, but for God's merciful providence, you may someday find yourself. If and when you do, I hope you will never fail because of what you do or do not do. But if you do experience failure, at least now you will know what to do about it.